# Inspiring Stories of Olympic Legends

## Frank Davis

# CONTENTS

# CONTENTS

# INTRODUCTION

The Olympics are a showcase of the human spirit and a celebration of the pursuit of excellence. Every four years, athletes from all around the world gather to compete against each other in a spirit of friendly competition and camaraderie. Many of these athletes are true legends in their respective sports, and their stories of perseverance, dedication, and triumph over adversity continue to inspire people of all ages.

In this book, we bring you the stories of 30 Olympic athlete legends from around the world. These athletes come from different countries and different eras, but they all share one thing in common: their remarkable achievements in their respective sports. From Sonja Henie, the Norwegian figure skater who won three consecutive Olympic gold medals in the 1920s and 1930s, to Ian Thorpe, the Australian swimmer who won five Olympic gold medals in the 2000s, these athletes have left an indelible mark on Olympic history.

Through their stories, we hope to inspire and motivate readers of all ages to pursue their dreams with determination and passion, to overcome obstacles, and to never give up in the face of adversity. These athletes are not just champions in their respective sports, they are role models and inspirations to us all. We hope that their stories will inspire you to reach for the stars and to never give up on your dreams, no matter how big or daunting they may seem.

# MICHAEL PHELPS

# FUN FACT ABOUT ME
## MICHAEL PHELPS

Michael Phelps was born on June 30, 1985 in Baltimore, Maryland, USA.

He is the most decorated Olympian of all time, with a total of 28 medals from five Olympic Games.

Phelps has also broken 39 world records during his career as a swimmer.

He began swimming at the age of seven, and by the age of 15, he had become the youngest male ever to make the U.S. Olympic swim team in 68 years

Phelps has struggled with mental health issues throughout his career, and has been open about his struggles with depression and anxiety.

He has been involved in several philanthropic efforts, including founding the Michael Phelps Foundation, which promotes water safety and healthy living for children.

Phelps retired from competitive swimming after the 2016 Rio Olympics, but has since come out of retirement and is training for the 2020 Tokyo Olympics, which were postponed to 2021 due to the COVID-19 pandemic.

Phelps has had several run-ins with the law, including two DUI arrests in 2004 and 2014, and has since become an advocate for mental health and substance abuse awareness.

Michael Phelps is one of the most decorated Olympic athletes of all time, with a total of 28 medals, including 23 gold medals. But his journey to success wasn't always easy.

Phelps was diagnosed with ADHD as a child, which made it difficult for him to focus in school. But he found an outlet in swimming, and started competing at a young age. He quickly showed a natural talent for the sport, and by the time he was a teenager, he was already breaking records.

But even as he dominated in the pool, Phelps faced challenges outside of it. He struggled with depression and anxiety, and turned to alcohol as a way to cope. In 2014, he was arrested for DUI, and was suspended from swimming for six months. It was a wake-up call for Phelps, and he sought help for his mental health issues.

Phelps returned to the pool with a renewed sense of purpose. He trained harder than ever before, and focused on his mental health as well as his physical training. In the 2016 Rio Olympics, he won five gold medals and one silver medal, bringing his career medal count to 28.

But Phelps' impact goes beyond just his accomplishments in the pool. He has become an advocate for mental health awareness, and has spoken openly about his struggles with depression and anxiety. He has also started the Michael Phelps Foundation, which promotes water safety and healthy living for children.

Phelps' story is an inspiration to all of us, because it shows us that even the greatest athletes face obstacles and challenges. But with hard work, determination, and a willingness to seek help, we can overcome those challenges and achieve great things. Phelps' commitment to mental health awareness and his philanthropic work also show us the importance of giving back to our communities.

So if you're facing challenges or obstacles on your own journey to success, remember that you're not alone. Look to Michael Phelps as an inspiration, and know that with hard work and perseverance, you can achieve anything you set your mind to.

# USAIN BOLT

# FUN FACT ABOUT ME
## USAIN BOLT

Usain Bolt was born in Sherwood Content, a small town in Jamaica, on August 21, 1986.

Bolt holds the world record for both the 100-meter and 200-meter sprints, with times of 9.58 seconds and 19.19 seconds, respectively.

Bolt's nickname is "Lightning Bolt," which was given to him because of his incredible speed on the track.

Bolt is a big fan of cricket, and has said that if he weren't a sprinter, he would want to be a professional cricket player.

Bolt is also a talented soccer player, and has even played in charity matches alongside professional soccer players like Lionel Messi and Cristiano Ronaldo.

Bolt is a big fan of dancehall music, and has even recorded his own music in Jamaica.

Bolt has a scoliosis, a curvature of the spine, which he says he has managed through exercise and core strengthening.

Bolt has been involved in several philanthropic efforts, including founding the Usain Bolt Foundation, which provides educational and cultural opportunities for children in Jamaica.

Usain Bolt is one of the greatest athletes of all time, and his journey to success is an inspiration to people around the world. From humble beginnings in Jamaica, Bolt rose to become a world record-breaking sprinter, and a cultural icon.

Bolt faced many challenges on his journey to success. He grew up in poverty, and struggled with scoliosis, a curvature of the spine. But he found an outlet in sports, and discovered that he had a natural talent for sprinting. He worked hard every day, and eventually became the fastest man in the world.

But Bolt's impact goes beyond just his accomplishments on the track. He has become a role model for children in Jamaica and around the world, inspiring them to pursue their dreams and work hard to achieve them. He has also used his platform to promote causes he believes in, including education, environmental sustainability, and social justice.

In 2012, Bolt founded the Usain Bolt Foundation, which supports children in Jamaica by providing access to education, sports, and cultural programs. The foundation has helped thousands of children, and has had a positive impact on the community.

Bolt's story shows us that with hard work, determination, and a willingness to overcome obstacles, we can achieve great things. He has also taught us the importance of giving back to our communities and using our success to make a positive impact on the world.

So if you're facing challenges or obstacles on your own journey to success, look to Usain Bolt as an inspiration. Know that with hard work and perseverance, you can achieve anything you set your mind to. And always remember to use your success to make a positive impact on the world around you.

# SIMONE BILES

# FUN FACT ABOUT ME
## SIMONE BILES

Simone Biles was born on March 14, 1997, in Columbus, Ohio.

She began practicing gymnastics at the age of six, and quickly showed a natural talent for the sport.

Biles is only 4'8" tall, which is smaller than the average height for a female gymnast.

She has won a total of 30 Olympic and World Championship medals, making her the most decorated American gymnast of all time.

Biles has a move named after her in gymnastics, called "The Biles," which is a double backflip with a twist.

Biles is an animal lover, and has a pet French Bulldog named Lilo.

She has used her platform as a gymnast to speak out on issues like mental health and sexual abuse in sports.

In 2019, Biles became the first woman in 70 years to win six U.S. all-around titles.

Simone Biles is one of the greatest gymnasts of all time, and her story is an inspiration to people around the world. From a young age, Biles faced many challenges and obstacles, but she never gave up on her dreams.

Biles was born into a family struggling with addiction, and was eventually placed in foster care. But she found solace in gymnastics, and quickly discovered that she had a natural talent for the sport. She worked hard every day, and eventually became a world-class gymnast.

Biles' accomplishments on the gymnastics floor are nothing short of incredible. She has won a total of 30 Olympic and World Championship medals, and has broken countless records along the way. But her impact goes beyond just her athletic accomplishments. She has used her platform as a gymnast to speak out on issues like mental health and sexual abuse in sports, and has become a role model for children around the world.

Biles has also faced her fair share of challenges and obstacles. She has dealt with injuries, self-doubt, and the pressure of being a world-class athlete. But she has always persevered, and has shown that with hard work and determination, anything is possible.

Biles' story is a reminder to all of us that no matter where we come from or what challenges we face, we have the power to achieve our dreams. She has shown us the importance of hard work, perseverance, and self-belief, and has inspired a generation of young people to pursue their passions and overcome their obstacles.

So if you're facing challenges or obstacles on your own journey to success, look to Simone Biles as an inspiration. Know that with hard work and determination, you can achieve anything you set your mind to. And always remember to use your success to make a positive impact on the world around you.

# CARL LEWIS

# FUN FACT ABOUT ME
## CARL LEWIS

Carl Lewis was born on July 1, 1961, in Birmingham, Alabama.

He grew up in a family of athletes, with his father being a track and field coach and his mother a hurdler.

Lewis won a total of 10 Olympic medals during his career, including 9 gold medals.

He was known for his incredible speed and jumping ability, and is widely considered to be one of the greatest track and field athletes of all time.

Lewis also had a successful career as an actor, appearing in movies like "Alien Hunter" and "Material Girls."

He is an avid supporter of animal rights, and has worked with organizations like PETA to promote animal welfare.

Lewis has been a vocal advocate for clean and fair sports, and has spoken out against the use of performance-enhancing drugs in athletics.

He is also a skilled businessman, and has been involved in ventures like real estate development and sports marketing.

Carl Lewis is a true inspiration to athletes around the world. Born into a family of athletes, Lewis had a passion for sports from a young age, and he worked tirelessly to become one of the greatest track and field athletes of all time.

Over the course of his career, Lewis won a total of 10 Olympic medals, including 9 gold medals, and set numerous world records. He was known for his incredible speed and jumping ability, and he inspired countless young athletes to pursue their dreams and strive for excellence.

But Lewis' impact goes beyond just his athletic accomplishments. He has used his platform as an athlete to advocate for important causes, including animal rights and fair play in sports. He has also been a role model for young people around the world, showing them the importance of hard work, dedication, and perseverance.

Lewis faced many challenges and obstacles along the way, including injuries and setbacks, but he never gave up on his dreams. He always remained focused on his goals, and he never lost sight of what was important to him. His story is a testament to the power of determination and resilience, and it is a reminder to all of us that we can overcome any obstacle if we work hard enough and believe in ourselves.

For children who aspire to be athletes, Carl Lewis' story is a source of inspiration and motivation. He shows them that with hard work, dedication, and a positive attitude, anything is possible. He also teaches them the importance of using their success to make a positive impact on the world around them, and to stand up for what they believe in.

In a world where young people are often faced with obstacles and challenges, Carl Lewis' story is a beacon of hope. He shows them that they have the power to achieve their dreams, and that they can use their talents and abilities to make a difference in the world. With his inspiring story, Carl Lewis continues to motivate and inspire young athletes around the world, and his legacy will continue to live on for generations to come.

# NADIA COMANECI

# FUN FACT ABOUT ME
## NADIA COMANECI

Nadia Comaneci was born on November 12, 1961, in Onesti, Romania.

She began gymnastics at the age of 6, and by the time she was 14, she had become one of the best gymnasts in the world.

At the 1976 Montreal Olympics, Comaneci became the first gymnast in history to score a perfect 10.

She won a total of 5 Olympic gold medals during her career, as well as numerous other international titles.

After retiring from gymnastics, Comaneci became an international ambassador for the sport, and she has worked tirelessly to promote gymnastics and inspire young athletes around the world.

Comaneci has been honored with numerous awards and accolades, including induction into the International Gymnastics Hall of Fame and the Laureus World Sports Academy.

She is also a successful businesswoman, with her own line of gymnastics equipment and a sports and fashion company.

Comaneci continues to be an inspiration to young athletes around the world, showing them that with hard work, dedication, and a positive attitude, anything is possible.

Nadia Comaneci is a true icon in the world of gymnastics, and her inspirational story is one that continues to inspire young athletes around the world.

Born in Romania in 1961, Comaneci showed an early talent for gymnastics. She began training at the age of 6, and by the time she was 9 years old, she had already won her first national championship. Her talent was undeniable, and it wasn't long before she became one of the top gymnasts in the world.

At the 1976 Montreal Olympics, Comaneci made history by becoming the first gymnast in history to score a perfect 10. She went on to win a total of 5 Olympic gold medals during her career, as well as numerous other international titles. Her grace, precision, and technical skill made her a favorite among fans and judges alike, and she inspired a generation of young gymnasts around the world.

Comaneci's impact on society goes beyond just her athletic accomplishments. She has used her platform as a world-renowned athlete to advocate for important causes, including children's rights and education. She has also been a role model for young people around the world, showing them the importance of hard work, dedication, and perseverance.

Comaneci faced many obstacles and challenges along the way, including injury, illness, and the pressures of competing at the highest level. But she never gave up on her dreams. She always remained focused on her goals, and she never lost sight of what was important to her. Her story is a testament to the power of determination and resilience, and it is a reminder to all of us that we can overcome any obstacle if we work hard enough and believe in ourselves.

For children who aspire to be athletes, Nadia Comaneci's story is a source of inspiration and motivation. She shows them that with hard work, dedication, and a positive attitude, anything is possible. She also teaches them the importance of using their success to make a positive impact on the world around them, and to stand up for what they believe in.

In a world where young people are often faced with obstacles and challenges, Nadia Comaneci's story is a beacon of hope. She shows them that they have the power to achieve their dreams, and that they can use their talents and abilities to make a difference in the world. With her inspiring story, Nadia Comaneci continues to motivate and inspire young athletes around the world, and her legacy will continue to live on for generations to come.

# PAAVO NURMI

# FUN FACT ABOUT ME
## PAAVO NURMI

He was born in 1897 in Turku, Finland, and grew up in a family of farmers.

Nurmi was known for his unique running style, which involved a straight back, high knee lift, and minimal arm movement.

He won a total of 9 Olympic gold medals and 3 silver medals in his career, making him one of the most successful Olympic athletes of all time.

Nurmi set 22 world records during his career, including records in the mile, 5000 meters, and 10,000 meters.

He was a vegetarian and believed that his diet played a key role in his success as an athlete.

Nurmi retired from competitive running in 1934, but continued to work in the sports industry as a coach and administrator.

He was a national hero in Finland and was awarded the Order of the White Rose of Finland, the country's highest civilian honor.

Nurmi passed away in 1973 at the age of 76, but his legacy as one of the greatest runners in history lives on.

Paavo Nurmi was born into a humble family of farmers in Turku, Finland in 1897. From a young age, he showed an interest in running and began competing in local races. Despite facing financial difficulties, Nurmi was determined to pursue his passion for running and began training rigorously.

In 1920, Nurmi represented Finland at the Summer Olympics in Antwerp, Belgium. He won his first gold medal in the 10,000 meter race, setting a new world record in the process. This was the beginning of a remarkable career that would see Nurmi win a total of 9 Olympic gold medals and set 22 world records.

Nurmi's success as an athlete had a profound impact on Finnish society. He became a national hero and inspired a generation of young people to pursue sports and physical fitness. His success also helped to put Finland on the map as a competitive force in international sports.

Despite his achievements, Nurmi faced his fair share of obstacles and challenges. In the 1924 Olympics in Paris, he was disqualified from the 1500 meter race for allegedly running out of his lane. This was a devastating blow for Nurmi, who had trained tirelessly for the event. However, he refused to let this setback define him and continued to compete at the highest level.

Nurmi's dedication to his sport and his unrelenting work ethic were a testament to his character. He was known for his intense training regimen and his ability to push himself to the limit during races. His competitive spirit and unwavering determination continue to inspire athletes around the world to this day.

Paavo Nurmi's legacy as one of the greatest distance runners of all time is a testament to the power of hard work and perseverance. His story serves as a powerful reminder to young people that with dedication, discipline, and a deep passion for what they do, they can overcome any obstacle and achieve their goals.

# JESSE OWENS

# FUN FACT ABOUT ME
## JESSE OWENS

Jesse Owens was born in Alabama in 1913 and grew up in Cleveland, Ohio.

He was named after a teacher who misheard his original name, J.C.

Owens was one of ten children and his parents struggled to make ends meet during his childhood.

He began running track in high school and quickly became one of the top sprinters in the state.

Owens attended Ohio State University where he set multiple records and won eight NCAA championships.

At the 1936 Olympics in Berlin, Owens won four gold medals in the 100 meter, 200 meter, 4x100 meter relay, and long jump events.

Owens faced discrimination and segregation in the United States, including being forced to use a separate entrance to a celebratory dinner in his honor.

After his athletic career, Owens became a successful businessman and continued to advocate for civil rights.

Jesse Owens is a true American hero, known not only for his incredible athletic achievements but also for his courage in the face of racism and discrimination. Born in Alabama in 1913, Owens grew up in a time when segregation and discrimination were rampant in the United States. Despite the many obstacles he faced, Owens became one of the greatest track and field athletes of all time.

As a high school student in Cleveland, Ohio, Owens quickly gained a reputation as a top sprinter. He went on to attend Ohio State University, where he set multiple records and won eight NCAA championships. In 1936, Owens made history at the Berlin Olympics, winning four gold medals in the 100 meter, 200 meter, 4x100 meter relay, and long jump events. His stunning performance was a significant blow to Nazi propaganda, which aimed to prove the superiority of the Aryan race.

Despite his Olympic success, Owens continued to face discrimination and segregation in the United States. He was not allowed to use the same entrances or facilities as white athletes, and he often had to sleep in separate hotels and eat in separate restaurants. Despite these challenges, Owens remained committed to his sport and to fighting for civil rights. He became a successful businessman and continued to advocate for equality throughout his life.

Jesse Owens' impact on society is immeasurable. His athletic achievements continue to inspire generations of young people around the world, and his courage in the face of adversity has made him an icon of the civil rights movement. His story is a powerful reminder that no matter what obstacles we face, we have the strength and determination to overcome them and achieve our goals. For children, Owens' story is a lesson in perseverance and resilience, showing that with hard work and dedication, anything is possible.

# EMIL ZATOPEK

# FUN FACT ABOUT ME
## EMIL ZATOPEK

Emil Zatopek was born in 1922 in Czechoslovakia and grew up in a working-class family.

He began running to improve his fitness while working as a factory worker during World War II.

Zatopek won his first gold medal in the 10,000 meter race at the 1948 London Olympics.

He went on to win two more gold medals at the 1952 Helsinki Olympics in the 5,000 and 10,000 meter races.

Zatopek was known for his grueling training methods, which included running in army boots and carrying a backpack filled with weights.

Zatopek was the first athlete to break the 29-minute mark in the 10,000 meter race, which he did in 1954.

Zatopek became a vocal opponent of the Communist regime in Czechoslovakia and was briefly imprisoned.

Zatopek died in 2000 at the age of 78, but his legacy as one of the greatest distance runners of all time lives on.

Emil Zatopek was a Czechoslovakian distance runner who became one of the most successful athletes in Olympic history. Born into a working-class family, Zatopek began running as a way to improve his fitness while working as a factory worker during World War II.

Zatopek's early career was marked by hard work and perseverance. He trained relentlessly, running long distances every day and using unorthodox methods like running in army boots and carrying a backpack filled with weights. Despite these challenges, Zatopek quickly emerged as a talented runner, winning his first gold medal in the 10,000 meter race at the 1948 London Olympics.

Zatopek's greatest achievements came at the 1952 Helsinki Olympics, where he won gold medals in the 5,000 and 10,000 meter races, as well as the marathon. This feat has never been repeated by another runner.

But Zatopek's impact on society went far beyond his impressive athletic accomplishments. He was known for his humble personality and his dedication to his country, and was an inspiration to his fellow Czechoslovakians during a time of political turmoil.

In fact, Zatopek became a vocal opponent of the Communist regime in Czechoslovakia after retiring from competition, and was briefly imprisoned for his views. But he never wavered in his belief in the power of sport to bring people together and promote peace and understanding.

Zatopek's story is one of hard work, perseverance, and dedication to a cause greater than oneself. He faced obstacles and challenges both on and off the track, but never lost sight of his goals or his desire to inspire others. His legacy as one of the greatest distance runners of all time lives on, and he continues to inspire and motivate children to success through his example of hard work, determination, and unwavering dedication to a cause greater than oneself.

# MARK SPITZ

# FUN FACT ABOUT ME
## MARK SPITZ

Mark Spitz was born in California in 1950 and began swimming at a young age.

He won his first Olympic gold medal at the age of 18, at the 1968 Mexico City Olympics.

Spitz won a total of 11 Olympic medals over his career, including nine gold medals.

He set 33 world records in swimming during his career.

At the 1972 Munich Olympics, Spitz won seven gold medals, breaking the record for most gold medals won in a single Olympics.

He retired from competitive swimming at the age of 22 after the 1972 Olympics.

He has worked as a television commentator for swimming events and appeared in several commercials and TV shows.

In 2019, Spitz received the Lifetime Achievement Award from the International Swimming Hall of Fame.

Mark Spitz is an Olympic legend and one of the most successful swimmers in history. His story is one of hard work, dedication, and perseverance, and it has inspired many people, young and old, to pursue their dreams.

Spitz began swimming at a young age and quickly showed talent in the sport. He trained hard, spending countless hours in the pool to perfect his technique and build his endurance. His hard work paid off when he qualified for the 1968 Mexico City Olympics at the age of just 18.

At the Olympics, Spitz won two gold medals, one silver, and one bronze, but he was not satisfied. He knew he could do better, and he set his sights on the 1972 Munich Olympics.

Over the next four years, Spitz trained tirelessly, pushing himself to new heights. He worked on his technique, his speed, and his mental toughness, determined to become the best swimmer in the world.

At the 1972 Olympics, Spitz stunned the world by winning seven gold medals, breaking the record for most golds won in a single Olympics. He became an instant celebrity, known not only for his incredible talent but also for his distinctive mustache, which he grew as a good luck charm.

Despite his success, Spitz faced challenges and obstacles along the way. He had to overcome injuries, setbacks, and doubts about his abilities. But he never gave up. He believed in himself and his abilities, and he continued to work hard, even when things got tough.

Spitz's impact on society goes beyond his athletic achievements. He has inspired countless people with his dedication, his work ethic, and his positive attitude. He has shown that with hard work and determination, anything is possible.

Today, Mark Spitz is a role model for young people around the world. His story is proof that with dedication, perseverance, and a positive mindset, anyone can achieve their goals and make their dreams a reality.

# LARISA LATYNINA

# FUN FACT ABOUT ME
## LARISA LATYNINA

Larisa Latynina won a total of 18 Olympic medals, including nine gold medals, five silver medals, and four bronze medals..

She was the first female gymnast to win nine Olympic gold medals.

Latynina is regarded as one of the most successful Olympians of all time.

She was born on December 27, 1934, in Kherson, Ukraine.

Latynina was a member of the Soviet Union's national gymnastics team for over a decade, from 1954 to 1966.

She won her first Olympic medal, a silver medal in the team competition, at the 1956 Summer Olympics in Melbourne, Australia.

After retiring from competition, Latynina went on to become a coach and judge.

She was inducted into the International Gymnastics Hall of Fame in 1998.

Larisa Latynina was born in Ukraine in 1934 and had a passion for gymnastics from a young age. She began training at the age of 11 and quickly rose through the ranks to join the Soviet Union's national gymnastics team. In 1956, at the age of 21, she competed in her first Olympic Games in Melbourne, Australia, winning a silver medal in the team competition.

Over the course of her career, Latynina competed in three Olympic Games, winning a total of 18 medals, including nine golds, five silvers, and four bronzes. She was the first female gymnast to win nine Olympic gold medals, and her record stood for over 40 years until it was broken by swimmer Michael Phelps.

Latynina was known for introducing new, difficult techniques to gymnastics, which helped propel the sport forward and inspire a generation of young gymnasts. She was a trailblazer for women's gymnastics, showing that women could compete at the highest levels of the sport and achieve great success.

Despite her success, Latynina faced many challenges throughout her career. She competed during a time when the Soviet Union and the United States were engaged in a bitter Cold War, and there was intense pressure to win at all costs. She also faced injuries and setbacks, including a serious ankle injury that nearly ended her career.

Through it all, Latynina persevered and remained committed to her sport. She retired from competition in 1966 and went on to become a coach and judge, passing on her knowledge and experience to the next generation of gymnasts.

Latynina's impact on the sport of gymnastics cannot be overstated. She paved the way for future generations of female gymnasts, showing them what was possible with hard work, determination, and a relentless drive to succeed. Her legacy continues to inspire and motivate young gymnasts around the world to this day.

# STEVE REDGRAVE

# FUN FACT ABOUT ME
## STEVE REDGRAVE

Steve Redgrave is the only rower to have won gold medals at five consecutive Olympic Games (from 1984 to 2000).

He won his first Olympic gold medal at the age of 22 in the coxed fours event at the 1984 Summer Olympics in Los Angeles.

Redgrave has won 9 World Rowing Championships, 3 Commonwealth Games gold medals, and multiple Henley Royal Regatta titles.

In 2000, at the age of 38, Redgrave won his fifth Olympic gold medal in the coxless fours event at the Sydney Olympics, becoming one of the oldest athletes to win an Olympic gold medal in rowing.

Redgrave has been a vocal advocate for diabetes research, having been diagnosed with type 2 diabetes in 1997.

He was knighted in 2001 for his services to rowing and charity.

Redgrave has also competed in the London Marathon and the Ironman Triathlon.

He was the final torchbearer at the opening ceremony of the 2012 Summer Olympics in London, lighting the Olympic cauldron at the Olympic Stadium.

Steve Redgrave is one of the greatest rowers of all time, with a career that spanned over two decades and saw him win five consecutive Olympic gold medals. His success in the sport is an inspiration to young athletes all around the world.

Redgrave's journey to becoming a champion rower was not an easy one. He suffered from a genetic condition called ulcerative colitis, which caused him to lose weight and become very ill. Despite this, he never gave up on his dream of becoming a world-class rower. He trained hard and worked tirelessly to overcome his illness and become one of the best in his sport.

Redgrave's early career was marked by a number of setbacks and disappointments. He competed in his first Olympics in 1984 but failed to win a medal. However, he did not let this discourage him. Instead, he used this experience as motivation to work even harder and improve his performance.

Redgrave's hard work and dedication paid off in a big way. He went on to win gold medals at the 1988, 1992, 1996, 2000, and 2004 Olympic Games, setting records and dominating his competition. His success in the sport helped to inspire a new generation of young rowers, many of whom looked up to him as a role model.

Redgrave's impact on society goes beyond just his success in rowing. He has used his platform as a world-class athlete to raise awareness and support for a number of causes, including cancer research and environmental conservation. He has also been an advocate for fitness and healthy living, inspiring countless people to take up rowing and other sports.

Through his hard work, dedication, and perseverance, Steve Redgrave has become a true inspiration to young athletes everywhere. His story shows that with enough determination and effort, anyone can achieve their goals and become a champion in their chosen sport.

# AL OERTER

# FUN FACT ABOUT ME
## AL OERTER

Al Oerter won the gold medal in the discus throw in four consecutive Olympic Games: 1956, 1960, 1964, and 1968.

He is the only track and field athlete to win the same event in four consecutive Olympics. Oerter set a world record in the discus throw four times during his career.

He competed in the 1980 Olympic Trials at the age of 43, but did not qualify for the team.

Oerter was also an accomplished artist and sculptor.

He was a devoted family man and often brought his wife and children with him to his competitions.

Oerter struggled with asthma and allergies throughout his career, but used his condition as motivation to work harder.

After retiring from competitive sports, Oerter became a motivational speaker and spoke to corporations and schools about overcoming obstacles.

He was inducted into the U.S. Olympic Hall of Fame in 1983.

Al Oerter, the legendary American discus thrower, is a true inspiration for aspiring athletes. From a young age, Oerter showed a natural talent for throwing, but his journey to becoming an Olympic gold medalist was filled with obstacles and challenges.

Early in his career, Oerter suffered from asthma and was told by doctors that he would never be able to participate in sports. However, he refused to let his condition hold him back and began training hard to overcome his physical limitations. Through dedication and hard work, he was eventually able to manage his asthma and become a successful athlete.

Oerter's hard work paid off when he won his first Olympic gold medal in the discus throw at the 1956 Melbourne Olympics. He went on to win three more gold medals in the same event at the following three Olympic Games, becoming the first athlete to win four consecutive Olympic gold medals in the same individual event.

Throughout his career, Oerter faced many challenges, including injuries and setbacks. However, he always remained focused on his goals and continued to train hard, even when faced with adversity. He inspired many people with his determination and perseverance, both on and off the field.

After retiring from competition, Oerter continued to inspire young athletes through his work as a coach and mentor. He also used his platform to raise awareness for asthma and advocate for athletes with disabilities.

In recognition of his many achievements, Oerter was inducted into the International Olympic Committee's Hall of Fame and was awarded the Presidential Medal of Freedom by President George W. Bush in 2005.

Oerter's story is a testament to the power of hard work, dedication, and perseverance. It serves as a reminder that with determination and a positive attitude, anything is possible. He is a true inspiration for young athletes who aspire to achieve greatness, and his legacy will continue to inspire generations to come.

# DALEY THOMPSON

# FUN FACT ABOUT ME
## DALEY THOMPSON

Daley Thompson won two Olympic gold medals in the decathlon, in 1980 and 1984. He set four world records in the decathlon during his career.

Thompson was known for his charisma and showmanship during competitions.

He was awarded the Member of the Order of the British Empire (MBE) in 1982, and then promoted to Officer of the Order of the British Empire (OBE) in 1986.

Thompson's nickname was "The Legend".

In addition to his athletic career, Thompson has worked as a television presenter and motivational speaker.

Thompson was inspired to pursue athletics after watching the 1968 Olympics in Mexico City on TV.

He is the only decathlete to have held the world, Olympic, Commonwealth and European titles simultaneously.

Thompson was forced to retire from athletics due to injury in 1992, but has since remained involved in the sport as a commentator and coach.

Daley Thompson is considered one of the greatest decathletes in history, having won two Olympic gold medals, three Commonwealth Games gold medals, and one European Championships gold medal. His career was characterized by his remarkable athletic abilities, strong work ethic, and his ability to overcome adversity.

Thompson began his career as a sprinter, but it wasn't until he switched to the decathlon that he found his true calling. His early training was unconventional, as he would often train in a nearby park, jumping over benches and doing pull-ups on lampposts. However, this unorthodox approach allowed him to develop his skills in a unique way and prepared him for the grueling events of the decathlon.

In the 1980 Moscow Olympics, Thompson won his first gold medal in the decathlon, setting a new world record in the process. Four years later, at the 1984 Los Angeles Olympics, he won his second gold medal in the decathlon, despite suffering from an injury to his thigh. His performance in LA is considered one of the greatest performances in Olympic history.

Thompson's impact on society went beyond his achievements in athletics. He was known for his charismatic personality and his ability to inspire and motivate others, both on and off the track. He was also an advocate for racial equality and spoke out against discrimination in sports.

Throughout his career, Thompson faced many obstacles and challenges, including injuries, setbacks, and a difficult training regimen. However, he never gave up and always pushed himself to be the best. His perseverance and determination are qualities that can inspire and motivate children to achieve their own goals and overcome their own obstacles.

Daley Thompson's legacy as one of the greatest decathletes of all time, combined with his inspiring personality and his ability to overcome challenges, makes him a true inspiration to young athletes everywhere.

# KIPCHOGE KEINO

# FUN FACT ABOUT ME
## KIPCHOGE KEINO

Kipchoge Keino was born on January 17, 1940, in Nandi Hills, Kenya.

He was the first Kenyan athlete to win an Olympic gold medal, which he won in the 1500m race at the 1968 Mexico City Olympics.

Keino was nicknamed "The Greatest Kenyan" and is considered a national hero in Kenya.

In the 1972 Munich Olympics, Keino won gold in the 3000m steeplechase, setting a world record in the process.

Keino also won silver in the 1500m race at the same Olympics, despite suffering from a gallbladder infection and a fever of 103 degrees Fahrenheit.

He founded the Kip Keino Foundation in 2002, which helps impoverished children in Kenya by providing education and athletic training.

Keino served as the chairman of the Kenyan Olympic Committee from 1999 to 2017.

In 2018, he was awarded the Olympic Laurel, which is the highest honor in the Olympic movement and recognizes outstanding contributions to sport and society.

Kipchoge Keino is a Kenyan distance runner who is widely considered to be one of the greatest middle-distance runners of all time. His impressive career has spanned over two decades, and he has inspired countless people with his dedication and perseverance. Here is an inspirational story about Kipchoge Keino.

Kipchoge Keino was born on January 17, 1940, in Kipsamo, Nandi District, Kenya. He was one of ten children, and his parents were poor farmers. Keino attended Kamasia Primary School and later, Kapsabet High School, where he began to show a talent for running. Keino used to run to and from school, which was about six miles away, and he quickly became known as one of the fastest runners in the area.

Keino's greatest accomplishment came in the 1968 Olympic Games in Mexico City. In the 10,000-meter race, he faced off against the favored Australian runner Ron Clarke. Keino trailed Clarke for much of the race, but with just two laps remaining, he made a move and passed Clarke, winning the race by a comfortable margin. Keino's victory in the 10,000-meter race was his first Olympic gold medal, and it made him an instant national hero.

Kipchoge Keino's impact on society is immeasurable. He has been an inspiration to countless people, not just in Kenya, but around the world. Keino's success on the track helped to put Kenya on the map as a running powerhouse, and he inspired a generation of Kenyan athletes to follow in his footsteps.

Kipchoge Keino faced many obstacles and challenges throughout his career. In the lead up to the 1968 Olympics, Keino was struggling with a serious gallbladder infection, and many people thought he would not be able to compete. However, he refused to let his illness hold him back, and he pushed through the pain to win his first Olympic gold medal.

Kipchoge Keino's story is a powerful inspiration for children all over the world. His dedication to his sport, his willingness to work hard, and his refusal to give up in the face of adversity are all qualities that children can look up to and learn from. Kipchoge Keino's legacy will continue to inspire future generations of athletes for years to come.

# FRANZ KLAMMER

# FUN FACT ABOUT ME
## FRANZ KLAMMER

Franz Klammer was born on December 3, 1953, in Mooswald, Austria.

Klammer started skiing at the age of 3 and joined the local ski club at the age of 5.

He won his first race at the age of 10 and was named to the Austrian national ski team at the age of 18.

Klammer won his first World Cup race in 1975 and went on to win 25 more races during his career.

He is best known for his performance at the 1976 Winter Olympics in Innsbruck, where he won the gold medal in the downhill skiing event.

Klammer has been inducted into numerous sports halls of fame, including the International Ski Racing Hall of Fame and the Austrian Sports Hall of Fame.

He has also worked as a commentator for ski races and has been involved in various charitable causes.

In 2018, Klammer was awarded the Olympic Laurel, the highest honor given by the International Olympic Committee, for his contribution to the Olympic movement.

Franz Klammer is a legendary Austrian skier who is widely regarded as one of the greatest downhill racers in history. He has inspired generations of athletes with his skill, determination, and sportsmanship. Franz Klammer was born in 1953 in Austria. He grew up in a family of skiers and started skiing at the age of three. He was a natural talent and quickly rose through the ranks. By the age of 16, he was already a member of the Austrian national ski team. He had his first big breakthrough in 1974 when he won the downhill at the junior world championships.

Klammer's greatest accomplishment came in the 1976 Winter Olympics in Innsbruck, Austria. He won the gold medal in the downhill race, which is considered the most prestigious event in alpine skiing. What made Klammer's victory even more remarkable was the fact that he was the underdog going into the race. He was up against some of the best skiers in the world, including the reigning world champion, and he was racing on his home turf, which added to the pressure. But Klammer rose to the occasion and delivered a performance for the ages. He attacked the course with fearless abandon, taking risks that other skiers wouldn't dare. He crossed the finish line with a time that was over a second faster than his nearest competitor, winning the gold medal and cementing his place in skiing history.

Klammer's victory in the 1976 Olympics was a defining moment for Austria. It was a moment of national pride and unity that brought the country together. Klammer became a national hero and a symbol of Austrian excellence. He inspired a generation of young skiers who looked up to him as a role model and an inspiration. Klammer's legacy still lives on today, and he remains a beloved figure in Austria and beyond.

Like all great athletes, Klammer faced his share challenges throughout his career. He suffered several injuries that could have ended his career, including a broken leg and a dislocated shoulder. But Klammer never gave up. He was determined to come back stronger and better than ever. He worked tirelessly to recover from his injuries, and he used his setbacks as motivation to push himself harder. Klammer's resilience and determination are a testament to his character and his unwavering commitment to excellence.

Klammer's story is an inspiration to children everywhere. His dedication, hard work, and never-say-die attitude are the qualities that children need to succeed in life. Klammer's story shows that anything is possible if you have the courage to pursue your dreams and the determination to overcome the obstacles that stand in your way.

# OLGA KORBUT

# FUN FACT ABOUT ME
## OLGA KORBUT

Olga Korbut was born on May 16, 1955, in Hrodna, Belarus (then part of the Soviet Union).

She first started training in gymnastics at the age of 8.

Korbut became famous at the 1972 Summer Olympics in Munich, where she won three gold medals and one silver medal.

Korbut's signature move on the balance beam was a backflip while grabbing her ankles.

She became a global icon of the sport of gymnastics and was often referred to as the "Sparrow from Minsk."

Korbut retired from gymnastics in 1977 at the age of 22.

In 1991, she moved to the United States and became a gymnastics coach.

Korbut was inducted into the International Gymnastics Hall of Fame in 1997.

Olga Korbut was born in Belarus in 1955, and from a young age, it was clear that she was destined for greatness. She began training in gymnastics at the age of 8, and by the time she was 11, she was already competing at the national level. In 1972, she burst onto the world stage at the Munich Olympics, where she won three gold medals and a silver, and captured the hearts of people all over the world with her youthful energy, athleticism, and infectious smile.

Olga Korbut is widely regarded as one of the greatest gymnasts of all time, and her accomplishments speak for themselves. In addition to her four Olympic medals, she won two World Championship titles, nine European Championship titles, and dozens of other international competitions. She is also credited with popularizing the sport of gymnastics around the world, and inspiring countless young girls to take up the sport.

Olga Korbut's impact on society cannot be overstated. In addition to her athletic accomplishments, she became a symbol of hope and inspiration for people all over the world, especially those living under repressive regimes. Her smile, her energy, and her indomitable spirit helped to remind people that there is always hope, and that even in the darkest of times, there is still beauty and joy to be found.

Despite her many accomplishments, Olga Korbut faced her fair share of obstacles and challenges along the way. As a child, she was often criticized and belittled by her coaches, who told her that she was too small, too weak, and too fragile to ever become a great gymnast. But Olga refused to give up, and instead, she worked tirelessly to improve her strength, flexibility, and technique. She also had to overcome a number of injuries and setbacks throughout her career, including a serious injury that almost prevented her from competing at the 1976 Montreal Olympics. But through it all, she remained determined, focused, and resilient, and she proved to the world that with hard work and perseverance, anything is possible.

To all the young girls and boys out there who dream of achieving great things, Olga Korbut is proof that anything is possible if you are willing to work hard, believe in yourself, and never give up. Her infectious energy, her relentless spirit, and her unwavering commitment to excellence serve as an inspiration to us all, and remind us that no matter what challenges we may face in life, we always have the power to overcome them and achieve our dreams. So, keep striving for greatness, keep pushing yourself to be the best that you can be, and never forget that with passion, determination, and a little bit of luck, anything is possible!

# NADIA PETROVA

# FUN FACT ABOUT ME
## NADIA PETROVA

Nadia Petrova was born on June 8, 1982, in Moscow, Russia.

Petrova was known for her powerful serve and aggressive baseline play.

Throughout her career, she won 37 WTA singles titles and 24 doubles titles.

She reached a career-high ranking of World No. 3 in singles in 2006.

Petrova also won two Grand Slam doubles titles and a mixed doubles title at the Australian Open in 2005.

In addition to her success on the court, she was also named the Russian Tennis Federation's Player of the Year four times.

Petrova was known for her philanthropic work and was awarded the WTA Humanitarian of the Year Award in 2006.

She retired from professional tennis in 2017.

Nadia Petrova is a former Russian professional tennis player who had an illustrious career spanning over two decades. She was born in Moscow, Russia, in 1982, and started playing tennis at the age of four. Petrova's family was very supportive of her career, and they even built a private tennis court for her to practice on.

Early in her career, Petrova was known for her explosive serve and powerful groundstrokes. She turned professional in 1999 at the age of 17, and her early years on tour were marked by a series of impressive performances. In 2003, she won her first WTA singles title at the Qatar Total Open, and over the next decade, she would go on to win another 12 titles in singles and 24 in doubles.

Petrova's key accomplishments include reaching a career-high ranking of world No. 3 in singles and No. 3 in doubles, winning two Grand Slam doubles titles (the French Open in 2012 and the US Open in 2004), and winning the silver medal in singles at the 2012 Olympics in London. She was also a member of the Russian team that won the Fed Cup in 2004 and 2008.

Off the court, Petrova has been involved in various charitable and philanthropic endeavors throughout her career. She has worked with several organizations to help children in need, including the Elena and Gennady Timchenko Charitable Foundation and the Maria Sharapova Foundation.

Despite facing several obstacles and challenges throughout her career, including injuries and personal setbacks, Petrova remained committed to her sport and continued to work hard to achieve her goals. She is an inspiration to young athletes everywhere, showing them that with hard work, dedication, and perseverance, anything is possible. Her legacy in tennis and her impact on society are a testament to her resilience and strength, and she will always be remembered as one of the greats of the game.

# MARTINA NAVRATILOVA

# FUN FACT ABOUT ME
## MARTINA NAVRATILOVA

Martina Navratilova was born in Prague, Czechoslovakia (now Czech Republic) in 1956. She became a US citizen in 1981.

Navratilova won 59 Grand Slam titles in singles, doubles, and mixed doubles, which is a record.

She won a total of 18 Grand Slam singles titles, including 9 Wimbledon championships.

Navratilova is known for her serve-and-volley playing style, which was highly effective on grass courts.

She was the world No. 1 tennis player for a total of 332 weeks, which is the most in tennis history.

Navratilova won a total of 167 singles titles and 177 doubles titles over the course of her career.

She was inducted into the International Tennis Hall of Fame in 2000.

She has written several books, including an autobiography titled "Martina."

Martina Navratilova is a tennis legend who has inspired many generations through her dedication, hard work, and sportsmanship. Her journey to success was filled with obstacles, but she never let them define her.

Martina Navratilova was born in Czechoslovakia and began playing tennis at the age of six. She showed great potential as a player and became a professional at the age of 18. Her early career was marked by consistent performances, but she struggled to win the big tournaments. It was only when she moved to the United States in the late 1970s that she began to realize her full potential.

Martina Navratilova is one of the greatest tennis players of all time. She won a total of 59 Grand Slam titles, which is a record for any player in singles, doubles, and mixed doubles. She was ranked World No.1 in singles for a total of 332 weeks, which is also a record. Martina won 167 singles titles and 177 doubles titles in her career. She is also known for her fierce rivalry with Chris Evert, which is considered to be one of the greatest in tennis history.

Martina Navratilova faced many obstacles and challenges throughout her career. She was initially rejected by the tennis establishment in Czechoslovakia because of her outspoken personality and was not allowed to play in many tournaments. She also faced discrimination for being openly gay, which made it difficult for her to find sponsors and endorsements. However, Martina persevered and continued to work hard, which led to her success on the court and paved the way for other athletes to be themselves.

In conclusion, Martina Navratilova's journey to success is a testament to the power of hard work, dedication, and perseverance. She never let her obstacles define her and instead used them as fuel to push herself even harder. Martina's legacy goes beyond her numerous titles and records and serves as an inspiration to all those who face challenges and adversity.

# EDWIN MOSES

# FUN FACT ABOUT ME
## EDWIN MOSES

Edwin Moses was born on August 31, 1955, in Dayton, Ohio, USA.

He is known for his domination in the 400-meter hurdles event, winning two Olympic gold medals and setting the world record four times.

Moses started his athletic career as a youth sprinter, but eventually turned to the 400m hurdles at Morehouse College.

He famously won 122 consecutive races in the 400m hurdles between 1977 and 1987, a feat that is unmatched in track and field history.

Moses also won three world championships and set the world record for the 400m hurdles at the 1976 Olympic Games in Montreal.

He was known for his unique style of hurdling, where he would take 13 strides between each hurdle rather than the traditional 14.

Moses was a vocal advocate for drug testing in sports and was a founding member of the United States Anti-Doping Agency. including founding the Laureus World Sports Academy and serving as chairman of the Laureus Sport for Good Foundation.

In 2000, Moses was inducted into the International Olympic Committee's Hall of Fame.

Edwin Moses was born in Dayton, Ohio in 1955. He was a talented athlete, excelling in several sports including basketball, football, and track and field. However, it was his natural ability for hurdling that would ultimately set him on the path to greatness. He competed for Morehouse College, a historically black college in Atlanta, where he set records and won championships. Despite this success, he had to face discrimination and obstacles due to his race, which would only fuel his drive to succeed even more.

Moses is widely considered one of the greatest hurdlers of all time. He won two Olympic gold medals in the 400-meter hurdles, in 1976 and 1984, and set the world record four times. He also won three World Championship titles and was unbeaten in the event from 1977 to 1987, during which time he won 122 consecutive races. Moses was inducted into the U.S. Olympic Hall of Fame, the Track and Field Hall of Fame, and the International Olympic Committee's Hall of Fame.

Moses had a significant impact on the sport of track and field, and his success inspired many young athletes to take up the hurdles. He also used his platform to speak out against doping in sports and was a vocal advocate for clean competition. Moses was also active in philanthropic work, founding the Edwin Moses Foundation, which works to empower and inspire youth through education, sports, and health initiatives.

Despite his incredible success on the track, Moses had to overcome many obstacles throughout his career. As a black athlete in the 1970s, he faced discrimination and prejudice, and his athletic achievements were often overlooked or downplayed. He also suffered a serious injury just weeks before the 1980 Olympics, which prevented him from competing at his peak. However, Moses never gave up and continued to train and work hard, eventually bouncing back to win gold in 1984. His perseverance and determination are an inspiration to all who face adversity.

Overall, Edwin Moses is a true icon of track and field, and his achievements and impact continue to inspire athletes and fans around the world. His story teaches us the importance of hard work, dedication, and resilience in the face of obstacles. As he once said, "The greatest pleasure in life is doing what people say you cannot do."

# JACKIE JOYNER-KERSEE

# FUN FACT ABOUT ME
## JACKIE JOYNER-KERSEE

Jackie Joyner-Kersee was born in East St. Louis, Illinois on March 3, 1962.

She grew up in poverty and had to share a bed with four of her siblings.

Jackie was a multi-sport athlete in high school and also played basketball, volleyball, and competed in track and field.

She attended the University of California, Los Angeles (UCLA) where she set records in the heptathlon and long jump.

Joyner-Kersee won six Olympic medals in her career, including three gold medals in the heptathlon and one gold medal in the long jump.

Jackie is a philanthropist and has created the Jackie Joyner-Kersee Foundation to provide programs that promote health, education, and leadership for young people.

She was named Sports Illustrated's "Greatest Female Athlete of the 20th Century" in 1999.

Jackie was inducted into the Olympic Hall of Fame in 2004.

Jackie Joyner-Kersee was born in 1962 in East St. Louis, Illinois. She grew up in a family of athletes and started competing in track and field events in high school. Joyner-Kersee attended the University of California, Los Angeles (UCLA) on a full athletic scholarship and became a three-time NCAA champion in the heptathlon. She went on to become one of the most successful athletes in Olympic history, dominating the heptathlon and long jump events.

Joyner-Kersee won six Olympic medals throughout her career, including three gold medals in the heptathlon and one in the long jump. She set world records in both events, with her heptathlon world record lasting for over 20 years. Joyner-Kersee was also a four-time world champion and a two-time Olympic bronze medalist.

Joyner-Kersee's success as an athlete has made her a role model and inspiration to many people around the world. She has used her platform to advocate for social justice, women's rights, and health and fitness initiatives. Joyner-Kersee founded the Jackie Joyner-Kersee Foundation, which aims to improve the lives of children in underprivileged communities through education and sports programs.

Despite her success, Joyner-Kersee faced many obstacles throughout her career. She had to overcome a difficult childhood in a low-income area and had to deal with injuries and health issues that threatened to derail her career. In 1988, she suffered a hamstring injury during the Olympic Trials and was told by doctors that she would not be able to compete in the Olympics. However, Joyner-Kersee refused to give up and worked hard to rehab her injury in time for the Olympics. She went on to win gold medals in both the heptathlon and long jump, setting a world record in the heptathlon in the process.

Joyner-Kersee's story is a testament to the power of perseverance and hard work. She overcame countless obstacles to become one of the most successful athletes in history, and continues to inspire and motivate people around the world. Her commitment to helping others and advocating for social justice makes her an important figure in both sports and society.

# CATHY FREEMAN

# FUN FACT ABOUT ME
## CATHY FREEMAN

Cathy Freeman was born on February 16, 1973, in Mackay, Queensland, Australia.

She was the first Aboriginal Australian to win a Commonwealth Games gold medal in 1990.

Freeman won a silver medal in the 400m at the 1996 Atlanta Olympics, setting a new Australian record of 48.63 seconds.

She won the 400m gold medal at the 2000 Sydney Olympics, becoming the first Australian Indigenous person to win an Olympic gold medal in an individual event.

Freeman was awarded the Laureus World Sports Award for Comeback of the Year in 2001 after coming back from injury to win gold at the Sydney Olympics.

She founded the Cathy Freeman Foundation in 2007, which aims to improve education outcomes for Indigenous Australian children.

Freeman was inducted into the Sport Australia Hall of Fame in 2005.

She was also inducted into the International Association of Athletics Federations Hall of Fame in 2018.

Cathy Freeman was born on February 16, 1973, in Mackay, Queensland, Australia. She started running at the age of five and showed exceptional talent at an early age. By the time she was 16, Freeman was already a national champion in her age group. She quickly rose through the ranks and made her international debut at the 1990 Commonwealth Games in Auckland, New Zealand, where she won a silver medal. Freeman's career took off from there, and she went on to become one of Australia's most successful athletes.

Freeman's most significant achievement came at the 2000 Sydney Olympics, where she won the gold medal in the 400-meter race. Her victory was especially significant for Australia, as she was the first Aboriginal Australian to win an individual Olympic gold medal. Freeman's win was also a powerful moment for reconciliation between Indigenous and non-Indigenous Australians. She retired from athletics in 2003 after winning two Commonwealth Games gold medals, two World Championships, and an Olympic gold medal.

Cathy Freeman's victory at the 2000 Sydney Olympics was a defining moment in Australian sporting history. Her win inspired a generation of young Australians, and she became a role model for Indigenous and non-Indigenous Australians alike. Freeman's victory was also a significant moment for the reconciliation movement in Australia, as she carried both the Aboriginal and Australian flags during her victory lap, symbolizing the unity of the two cultures.

Freeman faced many challenges and obstacles throughout her career. She struggled with depression and an eating disorder, which she has since spoken openly about. Freeman also faced significant pressure in the lead-up to the 2000 Sydney Olympics, as the eyes of the world were on her, and she was expected to win. Despite the pressure, Freeman remained focused and determined. She credits her success to her strong work ethic and her ability to stay focused on her goals.

In conclusion, Cathy Freeman's story is a testament to the power of hard work, determination, and resilience. Despite facing many obstacles throughout her career, Freeman remained focused on her goals and achieved incredible success. She is a true inspiration to young people all over the world, and her legacy will continue to inspire generations to come.

# WILMA RUDOLPH

# FUN FACT ABOUT ME
## WILMA RUDOLPH

Wilma Rudolph was born prematurely and weighed only 4.5 pounds. She had to wear a brace on her leg due to polio, and doctors thought she would never walk again.

Despite her physical challenges, Wilma Rudolph started running at the age of 7 and eventually became a talented sprinter.

She won three gold medals at the 1960 Rome Olympics, becoming the first American woman to win three gold medals in track and field at a single Olympics.

Rudolph was known for her unique style of starting races, known as the "Wilma start." She would start with her head down and her rear end high, and then burst off the blocks with explosive speed.

She set a world record in the 200m race in the 1960 Olympics, running it in just 24 seconds.

In 1961, Rudolph retired from competitive running and became a teacher and coach.

She was inducted into the U.S. Olympic Hall of Fame in 1983 and the National Women's Hall of Fame in 1994.

Rudolph was also a philanthropist and established the Wilma Rudolph Foundation, which helps young athletes with disabilities and disadvantaged backgrounds.

Wilma Rudolph was an American sprinter who overcame extreme adversity to become one of the most iconic and inspirational athletes of her time.

Wilma Rudolph was born prematurely in 1940 and weighed only 4.5 pounds. She was the 20th of 22 children in her family, and her parents were both farm laborers. At the age of four, Wilma contracted polio, which left her with a twisted left leg and a brace on it. Despite her disability, Wilma was determined to walk without her brace and did so by the age of nine. She started running in high school and soon became one of the fastest sprinters in the state of Tennessee.

In the 1960 Olympics, Wilma Rudolph won three gold medals in the 100m, 200m, and 4x100m relay, becoming the first American woman to win three gold medals in track and field. She set a world record in the 200m event, and her performance in the relay helped set another world record.

Wilma Rudolph's achievements broke down barriers for women and people of color in athletics. She became an inspiration to millions of people, especially those with physical disabilities. She used her platform to advocate for racial equality and women's rights and was a role model for young girls who aspired to be athletes.

Wilma Rudolph's journey to becoming an Olympic champion was not easy. She faced discrimination and segregation during the Jim Crow era, and her physical disability made it even more challenging for her to pursue her dreams. However, Wilma refused to let her circumstances define her, and she worked hard to become the best athlete she could be. She trained tirelessly and pushed through pain and setbacks, always with her eye on the prize. Her perseverance and determination paid off, and she became a legend in the world of track and field.

In conclusion, Wilma Rudolph's story is a powerful reminder that anything is possible with hard work and determination. Despite facing numerous obstacles and setbacks, she refused to let them stop her from achieving her goals. Her legacy continues to inspire people around the world, and she will always be remembered as one of the greatest athletes of all time.

# JEAN-CLAUDE KILLY

# FUN FACT ABOUT ME
## JEAN-CLAUDE KILLY

Jean-Claude Killy was born on August 30, 1943 in Saint-Cloud, France.

Killy started skiing at the age of two and was a natural talent, quickly advancing to competitions.

He won his first World Cup race in 1966 and went on to become a dominant force in the sport.

In addition to his Olympic success, Killy won three World Cup overall titles and was the first skier to earn over 100 World Cup points in a season.

After retiring from skiing, Killy became a successful businessman and served as a member of the International Olympic Committee.

Killy was named a Chevalier of the Legion of Honor in 1968 and was later promoted to Grand Officer in 2001.

Killy has been a prominent advocate for the environment and served as a Goodwill Ambassador for the United Nations Environmental Program.

In 2003, Killy was awarded the Olympic Order, the highest honor awarded by the International Olympic Committee.

Jean-Claude Killy is a legendary skier from France who achieved incredible feats in his career. His story is full of inspiration and motivation, making him a true role model for young athletes.

Jean-Claude Killy was born in 1943 in Saint-Cloud, France. He began skiing at the age of three and started to compete in local races as a teenager. In 1962, at the age of 19, he won his first major race at the French championships. This was just the beginning of a remarkable career that would see him become one of the greatest skiers of all time.

Killy's accomplishments are numerous and impressive. He won three gold medals at the 1968 Winter Olympics in Grenoble, France, in the downhill, giant slalom, and slalom events. He also won two World Cup overall titles in 1967 and 1968 and was the first skier to win all three disciplines in a single season. Killy retired from skiing at the age of 24, but his accomplishments continue to inspire generations of skiers.

Killy's impact on society extends far beyond the world of skiing. His success on the world stage inspired a generation of French athletes, and he became a national hero in France. Killy's legacy also includes his work as an Olympic official and advocate for youth sports. He was a member of the International Olympic Committee for many years and played a key role in the organization of the 1992 Winter Olympics in Albertville, France.

Like all great athletes, Killy faced many obstacles and challenges throughout his career. He suffered numerous injuries, including a broken leg in 1966 that nearly ended his career. However, he persevered through these setbacks and came back stronger than ever. Killy also faced pressure to perform at a high level, both from fans and from himself. Despite this pressure, he remained focused on his goals and achieved incredible success.

In conclusion, Jean-Claude Killy is a true legend of skiing and a role model for young athletes everywhere. His early career, key accomplishments, impact on society, and story of facing obstacles and challenges are all sources of inspiration and motivation for anyone who dreams of achieving greatness. By following in Killy's footsteps and working hard, anything is possible.

# VERA CASLAVSKA

# FUN FACT ABOUT ME
## VERA CASLAVSKA

Vera Caslavska was born on May 3, 1942, in Prague, Czechoslovakia.

She began gymnastics at the age of four.

She was the first gymnast to win the Olympic gold medal in the all-around competition twice, in 1964 and 1968.

Caslavska won a total of seven gold medals and four silver medals in the Olympics and World Championships.

In addition to her success in gymnastics, Caslavska was also a trained architect.

She used her platform as an athlete to speak out against the Soviet invasion of Czechoslovakia in 1968.

Caslavska retired from gymnastics in 1972 and became a coach.

She was inducted into the International Gymnastics Hall of Fame in 1998.

Vera Caslavska is widely regarded as one of the greatest gymnasts of all time. Her inspiring journey is an excellent example of how persistence and hard work can help you achieve your dreams. Vera Caslavska started gymnastics at the young age of six, and it quickly became clear that she was a natural talent. At age 15, she represented Czechoslovakia at her first major international competition, the 1958 European Championships. Though she didn't win a medal, she gained valuable experience and went on to become one of the most successful gymnasts in history.

Caslavska won a total of 22 medals at major international competitions, including seven Olympic golds. She won her first Olympic gold medal in 1964 in Tokyo, and then followed it up with three more golds at the 1968 Olympic Games in Mexico City. Her performances in 1968 were particularly memorable, as she won the all-around title, as well as golds in the balance beam and floor exercise. Caslavska was the first gymnast to win four golds at a single Olympic Games.

In addition to her achievements on the mat, Caslavska was also a powerful voice for democracy and human rights in her home country of Czechoslovakia. During the 1968 Olympics, she publicly protested the Soviet-led invasion of her country by turning her head away from the Soviet flag during the medal ceremony. This brave act made her a symbol of resistance against oppression and an inspiration to people around the world.

Despite her many successes, Caslavska faced her share of obstacles and challenges. She suffered from various injuries throughout her career, and even missed the 1966 World Championships due to a serious knee injury. However, she refused to let setbacks hold her back and always bounced back stronger than ever. Caslavska's story is a reminder that we all face challenges in life, but it's how we respond to them that truly matters.

In conclusion, Vera Caslavska is an inspiration to us all. Her incredible achievements as a gymnast, combined with her courage in standing up for what she believed in, make her a true hero. Her story shows that with hard work, determination, and a commitment to your values, anything is possible.

# DICK FOSBURY

# FUN FACT ABOUT ME
## DICK FOSBURY

Dick Fosbury revolutionized the high jump with his innovative "Fosbury Flop" technique, which involves jumping over the bar backwards.

Fosbury was initially ridiculed for his unusual technique, but he persevered and ultimately won a gold medal at the 1968 Olympic Games.

Fosbury attended Oregon State University, where he was a member of the track and field team.

Fosbury was inspired to develop his unique style after seeing another high jumper, Debbie Brill, jump backwards during a meet in 1963.

Fosbury's world record jump of 2.24 meters at the 1972 Olympics stood for seven years.

Fosbury has been inducted into multiple halls of fame, including the United States Olympic Hall of Fame and the National Track and Field Hall of Fame.

Fosbury has worked as an engineer and was involved in the development of the ski jump venue for the 2002 Winter Olympics in Salt Lake City.

Fosbury has been a vocal advocate for athlete safety and was instrumental in the development of modern high jump landing pads.

Dick Fosbury, a former high jumper from the United States, is an inspiration to all those who believe in thinking outside the box. Here's a look at his life, his accomplishments, and how he overcame adversity to become one of the greatest high jumpers in history.

Early in his career, Dick Fosbury was like any other high jumper, using the traditional "straddle" technique. However, he soon realized that this approach wasn't working for him, and he began experimenting with a new technique that involved jumping over the bar backwards, which eventually became known as the "Fosbury Flop." It was a revolutionary idea that changed the sport of high jumping forever.

Fosbury's key accomplishments included winning the gold medal at the 1968 Olympic Games in Mexico City with a jump of 7 feet, 4 1/4 inches, breaking the Olympic record and becoming the first person to clear the bar using the Fosbury Flop. He went on to win numerous other titles and set world records.

Fosbury's impact on society was significant, as his innovative technique not only revolutionized high jumping, but also inspired athletes in other sports to think creatively and outside the box. He showed that with hard work, determination, and the willingness to take risks and try new things, anything is possible.

Despite his success, Fosbury faced obstacles and challenges along the way. He was often ridiculed for his unorthodox technique, and many people thought he was crazy for even attempting it. But Fosbury didn't let these criticisms stop him. Instead, he used them as motivation to prove his critics wrong and achieve his goals.

To young athletes, Fosbury's story is a powerful reminder of the importance of perseverance, innovation, and self-belief. He showed that with hard work, dedication, and a willingness to take risks, anyone can achieve greatness. So, take a page from Fosbury's book and don't be afraid to think outside the box and pursue your dreams, no matter how unconventional they may seem.

# BONNIE BLAIR

# FUN FACT ABOUT ME
## BONNIE BLAIR

Bonnie Blair was born in Cornwall, New York, on March 18, 1964.

She started skating at the age of 2, and began speed skating at age 4.

Blair was a multi-sport athlete in high school, participating in soccer, track and field, and speed skating.

She attended university at Champaign-Urbana in Illinois, where she was a part of the track and field and speed skating teams.

Blair won her first Olympic medal, a bronze, at the 1988 Winter Olympics in Calgary.

She won a total of 5 Olympic gold medals, and is considered one of the greatest speed skaters of all time.

She set world records in the 500m and 1000m events during her career.

After retiring from speed skating, Blair has been an advocate for children's health and fitness, and works with the organization "Champions for Healthy Kids."

Bonnie Blair is a former American speed skater who has inspired millions of young athletes around the world with her dedication and hard work. Born in 1964 in New York, Blair started skating at a young age and soon developed a passion for the sport. She trained tirelessly, often waking up at 4:30 in the morning to practice before school. Her hard work paid off when she competed in her first Olympics at the age of 19.

Blair quickly became a dominant force in speed skating, winning her first gold medal in the 1988 Olympics in Calgary. Over the course of her career, she went on to win five Olympic gold medals and one bronze medal, becoming the most decorated American woman in Winter Olympic history. Blair also set multiple world records throughout her career, cementing her status as one of the greatest speed skaters of all time.

Beyond her impressive achievements on the ice, Blair has also had a significant impact on society. She has been a vocal advocate for education and has served as a role model for young girls and women around the world. She has worked with a number of organizations dedicated to promoting education and has spoken to countless young people about the importance of setting goals and working hard to achieve them.

Blair faced a number of obstacles and challenges throughout her career, including a battle with a respiratory illness that threatened to end her career. But she persevered, training even harder to overcome her illness and emerge as a stronger athlete. Her determination and resilience serve as an inspiration to young athletes everywhere, showing that with hard work and dedication, anything is possible.

In conclusion, Bonnie Blair's story is one of perseverance, dedication, and hard work. She overcame numerous obstacles and challenges to become one of the greatest speed skaters in history, and has used her platform to inspire young people around the world to pursue their dreams. Her story is a powerful reminder that with hard work and determination, anything is possible, and serves as an inspiration to young athletes everywhere.

# SERGEY BUBKA

# FUN FACT ABOUT ME
## SERGEY BUBKA

Sergey Bubka is considered the greatest pole vaulter of all time, holding the world record for 20 years.

He was born in Ukraine in 1963 and began pole vaulting at age 9.

Bubka won six consecutive World Championships from 1983 to 1997.

He was the first athlete to clear the height of 6.0 meters in pole vaulting.

Bubka competed in four Olympic Games, winning the gold medal at the 1988 Seoul Olympics.

Bubka competed in four Olympic Games, winning the gold medal at the 1988 Seoul Olympics.

Bubka was honored with the Prince of Asturias Award in Sports in 1991.

He has been inducted into the International Association of Athletics Federations Hall of Fame.

Sergey Bubka is a legendary pole vaulter from Ukraine who has inspired millions with his remarkable achievements in the sport. Sergey Bubka started his athletic career as a promising young athlete, showing great talent in pole vaulting. He quickly rose to fame, winning numerous national and international titles as a junior athlete. At the age of 19, he set his first world record in the event, a feat that would become his trademark throughout his career.

Throughout his career, Bubka set 35 world records in pole vaulting, making him one of the most successful athletes in the history of the sport. He won six consecutive world championship titles from 1983 to 1997, and also won the gold medal at the 1988 Olympic Games in Seoul. His dedication and passion for the sport made him a true champion, and an inspiration to many aspiring young athletes.

Bubka's remarkable achievements in pole vaulting have not only inspired millions of fans around the world, but have also helped to raise awareness and support for sports in his home country of Ukraine. He has been an active supporter of sports programs and charities in Ukraine, and has worked tirelessly to help young athletes achieve their dreams.

Bubka's journey to the top was not without its challenges. He faced numerous injuries and setbacks throughout his career, including a ruptured Achilles tendon that many thought would end his career. However, Bubka refused to give up, and worked tirelessly to recover and regain his strength. His determination and resilience helped him to overcome his obstacles and achieve his goals, inspiring many along the way.

To all the young athletes out there, remember that nothing is impossible if you work hard and believe in yourself. Sergey Bubka's story is proof that with dedication, passion, and a never-give-up attitude, anything is achievable. So, set your goals high, work hard to achieve them, and always remember that the only limits are the ones you set for yourself.

# IAN THORPE

# FUN FACT ABOUT ME
## IAN THORPE

Ian Thorpe was nicknamed "Thorpedo" due to his impressive speed and power in the water.

He won five Olympic gold medals and set numerous world records throughout his career.

Thorpe became the youngest-ever world champion in swimming at the age of 15.

He is known for his unique swimming technique, which involved a wide-arm stroke and a high leg-kick.

In addition to his swimming career, Thorpe has worked as a television commentator and written several books.

Thorpe was selected as one of Time Magazine's 100 most influential people in the world in 2000.

Thorpe is an advocate for mental health awareness and has spoken publicly about his struggles with depression and anxiety.

He has been a UNICEF Goodwill Ambassador since 2003 and has worked to improve access to education for children in underprivileged communities.

Ian Thorpe, also known as the "Thorpedo," is one of the most accomplished swimmers in history. He began swimming at a young age and quickly showed natural talent in the pool. As he grew older, he became more dedicated to the sport and started to train more seriously.

Thorpe's hard work paid off when he qualified for the 2000 Olympic Games in Sydney, Australia. There, he won three gold medals, becoming the youngest male swimmer to ever achieve such a feat. He continued to dominate in subsequent Olympic Games, winning a total of five gold medals and setting multiple world records.

Off the pool deck, Thorpe used his fame to make a positive impact on society. He became an advocate for various charitable causes, including indigenous rights and environmental conservation. He also openly spoke about his struggles with depression and mental health, helping to reduce stigma surrounding these issues.

However, Thorpe's success was not without its challenges. He faced intense pressure from the media and his own expectations, which led to a dip in his performance and a break from swimming. But with the help of his loved ones and a renewed focus on his mental and physical health, he was able to overcome these obstacles and return to the pool stronger than ever.

Thorpe's story serves as a powerful reminder to young people that success is not always easy, but it is possible with hard work, dedication, and support. Whether it's achieving a personal goal or making a positive impact in the world, Thorpe's story shows that anything is possible with perseverance and a willingness to overcome challenges.

# SONJA HENIE

# FUN FACT ABOUT ME
## SONJA HENIE

Sonja Henie was born in Oslo, Norway, in 1912.

She won her first national figure skating championship in Norway at the age of 10.

Henie became the youngest Olympic champion in figure skating history at the 1928 Winter Olympics in St. Moritz, Switzerland, at the age of 15.

She won gold at the next two Winter Olympics as well, in 1932 and 1936, becoming the only skater to win three consecutive Olympic gold medals in the discipline.

In addition to her Olympic victories, Henie also won 10 World Figure Skating Championships and 6 European Figure Skating Championships.

Henie was known for her signature skating move, the "Henie hop," in which she would jump and spin on one foot, landing on the opposite foot.

Henie was also a successful businesswoman, founding her own line of skating equipment and promoting ice shows around the world.

After retiring from competitive skating, she pursued a career in Hollywood, starring in several successful films.

Sonja Henie was born in Norway in 1912 and began figure skating at the young age of six. She quickly showed a natural talent for the sport and began competing at just eight years old. By the time she was 11, she was the Norwegian national champion.

Henie continued to dominate the sport, winning ten consecutive World Figure Skating Championships from 1927 to 1936, as well as three Olympic gold medals in 1928, 1932, and 1936. Her success on the ice made her an international superstar, and she even went on to become a successful actress in Hollywood.

But Henie's impact went beyond just her athletic achievements. She revolutionized the sport of figure skating by introducing new moves, such as the "Henie jump," and by wearing shorter skirts and white skating boots instead of the traditional black. Her bold fashion choices and innovative skating techniques inspired generations of figure skaters to come.

Henie faced her fair share of obstacles and challenges throughout her career, including criticism for her non-traditional style and the outbreak of World War II, which forced her to cancel her ice shows and return to Norway. But she persevered through it all, continuing to innovate and inspire others with her passion and dedication to her sport.

Today, Sonja Henie's legacy lives on as one of the greatest figure skaters of all time and a trailblazer for women in sports. Her story serves as a reminder to never give up on your dreams, even in the face of adversity, and to always strive to push the boundaries of what's possible.

# GREG LOUGANIS

# FUN FACT ABOUT ME
## GREG LOUGANIS

Greg Louganis was born on January 29, 1960, in El Cajon, California.

He started diving at the age of 9 and won his first National Championship at the age of 16.

He won a total of five Olympic medals, four of which were gold.

In the 1988 Olympics, Louganis hit his head on the diving board during a preliminary round, but he went on to win two gold medals in the same competition.

He is the only male diver in Olympic history to have won gold medals in both the springboard and platform events in two consecutive Olympics.

Louganis is known for his iconic reverse 2 1/2 somersault with 2 1/2 twists dive that he performed at the 1984 Olympics.

He was inducted into the International Swimming Hall of Fame in 1993 and the US Olympic Hall of Fame in 1985 and 2013.

After retiring from diving, Louganis pursued an acting career and appeared in several TV shows and movies, including "The Nanny" and "Watercolors."

Greg Louganis is widely regarded as one of the greatest divers of all time, having won multiple Olympic gold medals and world championships. However, his journey to success was not without its challenges and obstacles.

Early in his career, Louganis struggled with bullying and discrimination as a gay athlete. Despite these difficulties, he remained determined to pursue his passion for diving and become the best athlete he could be. He worked hard to perfect his technique and developed a reputation for performing some of the most difficult dives in the sport.

Louganis' accomplishments are numerous and impressive. He won a total of five Olympic medals, including four gold medals, and also claimed multiple world championship titles. He set numerous records during his career and is widely regarded as one of the greatest divers in history.

In addition to his achievements in the sport of diving, Louganis has also been an advocate for the LGBTQ+ community and has used his platform to raise awareness and promote equality. He has been a vocal supporter of organizations like the Human Rights Campaign and has used his own experiences to inspire others.

Despite facing many challenges throughout his life and career, Louganis has always remained focused on his goals and determined to succeed. His dedication and hard work have not only led to great achievements in the sport of diving, but also to making a positive impact on society.

To young people today, Louganis' story serves as a reminder that it's possible to overcome obstacles and achieve great things, even in the face of adversity. His determination and perseverance are an inspiration and a testament to the power of hard work and resilience.

Printed in Great Britain
by Amazon

36762806R00076